THE VOYAGE OF
COLUMBUS

Rupert Matthews

Illustrated by Tony Smith

The Bookwright Press
New York • 1989

Great Journeys

The Conquest of Everest
The First Men on the Moon
The First Transatlantic Flight
The First Voyage Around the World
The Race to the South Pole
The Travels of Marco Polo
The Voyage of Columbus
The Voyage of the Beagle

Cover *Christopher Columbus is one of history's best-known explorers. He sailed through unknown waters and documented many lands that had not previously been recorded.*

Frontispiece *A modern replica of a Spanish warship from the time of Columbus.*

First published in the
United States in 1989 by
The Bookwright Press
387 Park Avenue South
New York, NY 10016

First published in 1989 by
Wayland (Publishers) Limited
61 Western Road, Hove
East Sussex BN3 1JD, England

© Copyright 1989 Wayland (Publishers) Limited

Typeset by Lizzie George, Wayland
Printed in Italy by G. Canale & C.S.p.A., Turin

Library of Congress Cataloging-in-Publication Data
Matthews, Rupert.
  The voyage of Columbus / by Rupert Matthews.
  p. cm. — (Great journeys)
  Bibliography: p.
  Includes index.
  Summary: An account of the first two voyages of Christopher Columbus by which he reached the unknown continents of the Americas, the "New World."
  ISBN 0–531–18301–7
  1. Columbus, Christopher—Juvenile literature. 2. Explorers—America—Biography—Juvenile literature. 3. Explorers—Spain—Biography—Juvenile literature. 4. America—Discovery and exploration—Spanish—Juvenile literature. [1. Columbus, Christopher. 2. Explorers. 3. America—Discovery and exploration—Spanish.] I. Title II. Series
  E118.M27 1990
  970.01'5--dc 19   89-30843
                                                          CIP
                                                           AC

Contents

Before Columbus

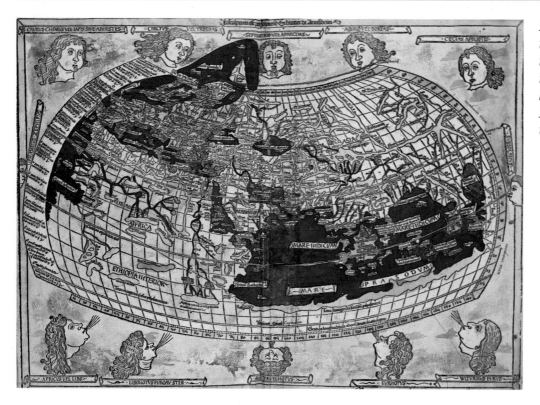

Left *A map of the world that was published in the German city of Ulm in 1486. It shows the lands known to Europeans before the voyages of Columbus.*

Christopher Columbus set sail on his first great voyage into unexplored waters on August 3, 1492. His journey opened up a vast new area of the world to European travelers, including the West Indies, the South American continent and Central America. Even at the time, the voyages of Columbus were recognized as outstandingly important. However, due to a lack of knowledge of world geography, nobody was quite sure exactly what lands he had found.

Before Columbus set sail, various ideas about the world were popular in Europe. One of the most popular was that there was only one landmass, which consisted of three continents – Europe, Asia and Africa. Only a few islands, such as the Canaries and Iceland, were thought to lie in the ocean that surrounded it. Even these three continents had not been fully explored. Nobody knew how far south Africa extended, or the size of the continent of Asia.

Only a very few Europeans had traveled in Asia. These travelers, who included Marco Polo, had been too busy trading, or escaping from bandit attacks, to have time to draw accurate maps. Some scholars thought that the Asian continent was only a little larger than Europe, while others were certain that it stretched over half the globe.

Above *Marco Polo, the Italian merchant who visited China in the thirteenth century and whose writings influenced Columbus' ideas about the world.*

Another popular idea was that there were more than three continents. It was thought that as there was so much land in the areas known to Europeans, there must be plenty of land elsewhere. Some people believed that a huge unknown continent lay somewhere south of the Equator. Others thought that it was situated in the ocean that separated western Europe from eastern Asia.

Virtually the only fact upon which scholars agreed was that the Earth was round. Even this idea led to serious disagreements because nobody was sure how large the world really was. Some thought the circumference of the Earth was 32,000 km (19,885 mi), others that it was 43,000 km (26,270 mi). The actual figure is 40,008 km (24,861 mi). Some people did not even agree that the world was round. The majority of ordinary Europeans (including many sailors) still believed that the world was flat and was centered around the ancient city of Jerusalem.

Some of the doubts concerning world geography were solved during the fifteenth century. Portuguese merchants sailed down the coast of Africa, trading with the local people for gold and ivory. It was hoped that if they sailed far enough to the south, they would be able to pass around Africa and continue to Asia. However, these voyages were long and difficult. Christopher Columbus hoped to change this situation.

Left An illustration from the time of Columbus showing ships in Lisbon Harbor. Lisbon was a busy port, used by many merchant ships and by explorers sent out by the King of Portugal.

The Vision of Columbus

Christopher Columbus was born in the Italian city of Genoa sometime between 1435 and 1451. His father was a weaver, as were most of his relatives. At the time, Genoa was the center of a thriving merchant trade. Genoese ships sailed throughout the Mediterranean, and as far north as Britain.

At the age of fourteen, Columbus was sent by his father on a business voyage. From the beginning, Columbus fell in love with the sea. He loved sailing and enjoyed visiting foreign ports. For several years he worked as a merchant, sailing to places such as Naples, Tunisia, Lisbon, Marseilles, Carthage, Cyprus and Sardinia. Genoa and Venice were at war when, in 1476, a Genoese fleet in which Columbus was sailing met some Venetian ships off the coast of Portugal. In the battle that followed, his ship sank and he had to swim 9 km (5½ mi) to shore.

Columbus made his way to Lisbon, where his younger brother Bartolomeo ran a map-making business. Columbus joined his brother's business. As part of his job, he sailed to Iceland, the Azores

Above *No portrait of Columbus dating from his lifetime has survived. This Italian painting, however, was produced only a few years after his death and is probably a good likeness.*

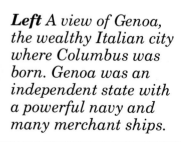

Left *A view of Genoa, the wealthy Italian city where Columbus was born. Genoa was an independent state with a powerful navy and many merchant ships.*

and the Canaries, and read many books about geography and about travelers who had journeyed to distant lands. From these books he learned of the theory that Asia lay to the west of Europe. As a merchant, Columbus was aware of the wealth of China and India. Any captain who managed to sail west to Asia could obtain great riches. Columbus sat down to calculate if such a voyage would be possible.

He decided, by studying books and maps, that the Earth had a circumference of 32,000 km (19,885 mi). He read about the journeys of the Venetian traveler Marco Polo and the Englishman Sir John Mandeville, who had visited China. From their journals, Columbus calculated the distance eastward from Europe to Asia to be 24,000 km (15,000 mi). Marco Polo had written that Japan lay 3,000 km (1,900 mi) east of China. Columbus decided that Japan was 5,000 km (3,100 mi) west of Europe. In fact the distance is 18,000 km (11,185 mi).

As an experienced seaman, Columbus knew that a voyage of 5,000 km (3,000 mi) was possible. From voyages in the Atlantic, he had learned that winds blow steadily west from the Canaries and east to the Azores. He thought that he could rely on winds to carry him west if he started from the Canaries. In order to come home, he need only sail north to find the east winds. As he searched for evidence to

Above and left
Fifteenth-century navigational equipment was very primitive. Both the sighting stick (above) and the astrolabe (left) were used to determine latitude; they depended on taking sightings from the sun, and on cloudy days they could not be used.

support his ideas, Columbus spoke to sea captains. He learned of wooden statues and tree trunks washed ashore on the Azores that had come from the west. Columbus was convinced that he could sail a ship to Asia by heading west. However, he did not have enough money to pay for the voyage. In 1484 he set about finding funds to allow him to make his journey.

At the Spanish Court

In 1484 Columbus took his plans to King John II of Portugal. The king was already paying for expeditions along the coast of Africa, and Columbus hoped he would also pay for a westward voyage. King John called together a committee of geographers to study Columbus' proposal. They pointed out that he was mistaken about the size of both the Earth and Asia. They told King John that he should not support Columbus. However, the king decided to send a ship of his own on a secret mission to the west. It returned without finding anything except empty ocean. When Columbus learned of this trickery he left Portugal.

Columbus asked for money from the Spanish court. King Ferdinand of Aragon and Queen Isabella of Castile had recently married, combining the wealth of their two kingdoms. They had sponsored a conquest of the Canaries, and Columbus hoped that these rich, adventurous monarchs would pay for his ships.

Columbus quickly persuaded the Duke of Medina Celi and other Spanish noblemen that a westward voyage to China was possible. They arranged for Columbus to meet Ferdinand and Isabella. In May 1486, Columbus explained his plans to the king and queen. They were impressed by his ideas

and excited by the possibility of trading with a nation as rich as China. However, Ferdinand and Isabella were at war with the Moorish state of Granada. They had little spare money for risky voyages and were investing in only the best ideas put before them. Columbus' ideas and calculations were sent to a group of geographical experts for inspection. Once again he had to justify his request and explain his ideas.

A nineteenth-century painting showing Columbus meeting Queen Isabella. Isabella was greatly impressed by Columbus and supported his requests for money and ships.

Above *An engraving of Isabella and Ferdinand, rulers of the combined kingdom of Castile and Aragon.*

Right *The Court of Lions in the beautiful Alhambra Palace in the city of Granada. Granada was the last Moorish stronghold in Spain to be captured by the Christian monarchs.*

After more than a year the commission had still not replied to his proposal. Columbus became very impatient and traveled to Portugal to see his brother Bartolomeo. Columbus once again asked King John for funds, but was turned down. Bartolomeo then offered to travel to England and France in search of money while his brother returned to Spain. In 1490 the Spanish experts finally replied. They had come to the same conclusion as the Portuguese committee: Columbus had got his figures wrong. However, by this time Columbus had gained the support of Queen Isabella and many important nobles.

In the autumn of 1491, Ferdinand and Isabella were with their army in front of the city of Granada. They summoned Columbus to them. The king and queen refused to tell him whether they would fund him while they were still at war.

Granada was captured in January 1492. The war was over, but there was still no sign of funding for Columbus. In disappointment, Columbus collected his maps and started out for Paris. But Columbus did not travel for long before he heard a horse galloping behind him. It was a royal messenger. Ferdinand and Isabella had agreed to give Columbus money for his ships.

Leaving Port

When he returned to court, Columbus was told that he would be able to make his voyage. However, he was involved in long talks about how much money he would be given for ships and what his rewards would be if he found China. These continued for several months, but finally agreement was reached.

Queen Isabella and a group of noblemen provided enough money to buy and equip three small ships. Columbus was not to be paid anything for the voyage unless he succeeded. But the rewards of success were rich and lavish. Columbus was to be viceroy of any lands he discovered. He was to be admiral of all Spanish ships that sailed to the lands he had visited. He was to take one tenth of all the gold, silver, jewels and pearls that might be found in the new lands. He was to be supreme judge of all disputes in these lands. Finally, he was allowed to invest money in any trading mission to be set up and take a share of the profits. If he succeeded in finding China, Columbus would be a very rich man.

On May 12, 1492, Columbus set out for the port of Palos, where he intended to find his ships and men. When the sailors and merchants at Palos saw Columbus' royal instructions and his money

they were eager to help. But when he told them of his mission they were less enthusiastic. Such a long voyage would be extremely dangerous, and none wanted to risk their lives or their ships. After several weeks, two brothers, Martin and Vincente Pinzon, came forward. They said that not only would they sell Columbus their ships but they would go with him as well. After this, other merchants came forward to offer stores and equipment.

The ships that Columbus took on his voyage were typical small merchant ships of the time. The *Santa Maria* was about 30 m (98 ft) long and had three decks. This ship was of a type known as a caravel. It had three masts, of which the center one was by far the highest, and tall bows and stern. Built as a trading ship, the *Santa Maria* could carry a heavy load but sailed slowly. The *Pinta* was slightly smaller and had decks at either end; in the center she was open to the elements. The smallest ship was the *Nina*, which was less than half the size of the *Santa Maria*. The *Nina* lacked deck and storage space, but was the fastest of the three vessels.

Having finally obtained his ships, Columbus stocked them with everything they would need on their long voyage. Various trade goods were also

Below Columbus bought his ships at Palos, where he stocked them with enough supplies and equipment to last through the long voyage.

loaded as presents for any monarchs they might meet. Ninety sailors were hired, together with a surgeon, a royal inspector, a few soldiers, cooks and servants. On August 3, 1492, the ships left harbor. Many men thought they would never see home again. On shore, relatives wept and prayed. It was not a happy start to the voyage.

On the High Seas

Left *The beautiful bay of San Sebastian, where Columbus anchored to repair the rudder of the* Pinta. *The modern town, and the sixteenth-century fortress on the headland to the left, are built on the sites of much earlier structures.*

Soon after leaving port, the rudder cable of the *Pinta* snapped. When Martin Pinzon, the captain of the *Pinta*, began to repair the damage he found the the cable had been cut deliberately; it seemed somebody on board did not want to risk the voyage into the unknown. Captain Pinzon could only patch the damage; he needed to reach a port to repair the rudder properly. Columbus changed course in order to stop at the Canaries.

The ships put in at San Sebastian on the island of Gomera. For three weeks Columbus waited for the *Pinta* to be repaired. He took advantage of the delay to buy fresh stores. A fisherman arrived and said that he had seen a Portuguese fleet nearby. Columbus thought that this

fleet had been sent to keep him from starting his voyage. On September 6, he set sail to escape from the Portuguese, but suddenly, the wind dropped. For three days Columbus' ships drifted with the currents within sight of the

Below *A map of the Canary Islands, showing the principal Spanish settlements.*

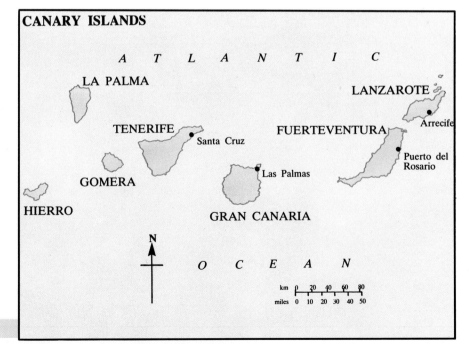

Canaries. Some sailors said that this calm was a sign from God that they should not sail.

On September 9, a wind blew up. At last Columbus was heading west. Knowing that the men might want to return home if they did not find land, Columbus began to trick them. He kept two different logs. In one, which he kept locked away in his cabin, he recorded the distance sailed and other observations. In the second, which he showed to the men, Columbus lied and wrote down shorter distances than they had actually covered. Columbus did not want the men to lose heart as the days went by, and land had still not been sighted.

As they sailed farther west, Columbus noticed something strange. For centuries, European sailors had known that the Pole Star always appeared exactly to the north. But his observations now showed the Pole Star to be some distance from north as indicated by the compass. Columbus did not know that the magnetic north of the compass is some distance from the North Pole. However, he kept an accurate record of the variation, which proved invaluable to later transatlantic travelers. Day after day, the ships sailed on across the ocean. Each day was very much like the one before. A steady breeze blew from the west, and the ships sailed steadily across the calm sea. Columbus was happy because the voyage was progressing well, but his men were not content. Trouble was brewing.

Below *Columbus writing up his log in his cabin on board the* Santa Maria. *Columbus kept two logs on his voyage, one that he showed to the sailors, and one that he kept secret.*

The Mutiny

Many of the men on Columbus' ships had not really wanted to sail on the voyage at all. Some had signed on as crew members to escape prison, others because they had been ordered to do so by royal decree. These men were frightened by the idea of a long voyage into unknown waters. They noticed every sign of approaching disaster and became increasingly unhappy. They began to try to make the rest of the men want to return home as well.

About 700 km (435 mi) from the Canaries, wreckage from a large ship was seen; the broken wood had obviously been in the water for some time. The sailors thought this proved that great dangers lay ahead. A few days later, on September 18, seaweed was seen floating on the ocean. Such weed grew only on rocks. The sailors were convinced that they would run aground and be wrecked unless Columbus stopped the ships. Columbus threw a weight on a line overboard and when it failed to hit bottom, the men agreed to sail on.

However, the sailors were clearly far from happy. One of them remembered tales of the sunken city of Atlantis, which was said to wreck any ships that passed near it. Once again Columbus tried to find the ocean bed with a lead weight.

On September 21, the wind died down. The ships were becalmed on water that was almost solid with seaweed. For three days there was no wind. When a breeze finally did arrive it was not strong enough to drive the ships through the seaweed. The men began to wonder if they would ever escape. They called the area *Sargaco*, which means "sea plants." To this day the region is called the Sargasso Sea. The vast amounts of seaweed are brought there by sea currents, but Columbus' men did not know why the seaweed was covering the ocean. They thought it was an evil place.

On September 25, huge waves rocked the ships, despite the fact there was no wind. The sailors became convinced they were in dangerous waters. Columbus and the other officers assured the crew that such happenings were common in open ocean. The sailors, most of whom had never sailed far from home, believed Columbus. They obeyed orders simply because they trusted the officers.

On October 6, the calm was shattered. Captain Pinzon argued openly with Columbus. He did not believe the log Columbus had shown to the sailors. He thought the fleet had traveled much farther than Columbus had admitted. According to Pinzon's measurements, they should have reached Japan some days earlier. Columbus managed to calm Pinzon by agreeing to sail southwest, in the direction in which birds had been seen to fly past the ship.

On October 10, the anger of the crew of the *Santa Maria* boiled over. They confronted Columbus and demanded to go home. Columbus tried to persuade them to carry on by promising them rewards. He showed them a fresh branch with berries on it that had been found that morning. The men were unmoved. Finally, Columbus agreed to turn for home if no land were sighted within three days.

15

Land!

On October 11, several land birds were seen flying around the masts of Columbus' ships, and a piece of wood carved into a strange shape was fished out of the sea. Columbus was convinced that land was not far away. By dusk nothing had been seen, but Columbus ordered the ships to drop anchor lest they run aground in the dark.

At ten that night, Columbus saw a light to the southwest. He pointed the light out to crew members Pedro Guttierrez and Rodrigo Sanchez, who both saw it. The light seemed to be moving around as if it were being carried by a man or horse. The *Pinta* pushed forward in the direction of the light. At two o'clock in the morning of October 12, a sailor named Rodrigo de Triana sighted land. When he heard the news Columbus fell to his knees. He had found land where he had been told there was none.

Below *The first sighting of land was made from the* Pinta *by the lookout, Rodrigo de Triana, early on the morning of Friday, October 12.*

When dawn broke, the sailors saw a small island ahead of them. Its green forests reached down to sandy beaches. Warm breezes stirred the leaves, and flowers bloomed in the greenery. As Columbus prepared to land, a group of people came out of the forest. They stood on the beach and stared at the ships. Columbus, the Pinzon brothers and a large group of sailors clambered into boats to land and claim the island for Spain. Columbus had dressed in his finest suit. When he saw the people on shore, he buckled on his armor and sword in case there was trouble. Many of the other sailors also carried weapons to protect them.

In the early morning light Columbus stepped ashore. Watching the crowd nervously, they unfurled the flag of Spain, and Columbus proclaimed himself viceroy of the island. He named the island San Salvador, but it has also been called Watling Island. It lies in the heart of the Bahamas, off the southeast coast of Florida.

Columbus then approached the group of people, keeping a grip on his sword in case they were dangerous. In fact they were friendly. They were amazed by the ships and clothes of the Spaniards. When Columbus gave them a few trinkets, they seemed very happy. Then they ran off. Because he thought he was in the East Indies, now known as the Philippines, Columbus called these people Indians.

The Spaniards set about exploring the island. They found that it was covered with forests, through which ran many small streams. It seemed that they had found a rich land. Next day the islanders returned in great numbers. Some of their chiefs wore small ornaments made from gold. Columbus eagerly asked, using sign language, where the gold had come from. The islanders pointed southeast and told Columbus about another, much larger island, which was situated nearby.

Columbus set sail again and steered southeast. Here he found another island, where the local people repeated that the gold came from a large island farther off. Columbus set sail again.

Below A contemporary illustration showing Columbus landing in the New World and erecting a large wooden cross as a thanksgiving to God for his safe ocean crossing.

Exploring the Islands

For more than two weeks Columbus sailed among the islands of the Bahamas. At each island he stopped and went ashore to meet the people. Using sign language he asked them questions and tried to understand their answers. Columbus was convinced that he had reached the islands off the coast of China that had been recorded by Marco Polo. He wanted to discover where the mainland was to be found. The islanders indicated that a large land lay to the south, so Columbus continued to sail in that direction.

On October 28, he finally reached a coastline that stretched out of sight. He

Above *A typical beach scene in the West Indies.*

Below *A map of the Bahamas and Cuba.*

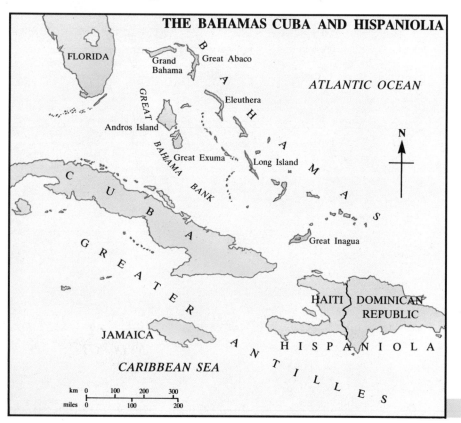

THE BAHAMAS CUBA AND HISPANIOLIA

FLORIDA

Grand Bahama

Great Abaco

ATLANTIC OCEAN

Eleuthera

Andros Island

GREAT

Great Exuma

Long Island

BAHAMA BANK

CUBA

N

GREATER

Great Inagua

HAITI   DOMINICAN REPUBLIC

JAMAICA

H I S P A N I O L A

ANTILLES

CARIBBEAN SEA

| km | 0 | 100 | 200 | 300 |
| miles | 0 | | 100 | 200 |

turned first west, then east. There seemed to be no end to the coast, and Columbus was certain that he had reached China. In fact, he had found Cuba. One thing puzzled Columbus. Instead of the rich temples and prosperous towns described by earlier visitors to China, he found only small villages and poor peasants. Though there was little gold and silver, Columbus found many things that were new to him, such as iguanas, parrots, songbirds, pineapples, tobacco, corn and sweet potatoes. Columbus carefully collected samples of these to take home. On November 21, a strong wind blew up and drove the *Pinta* away to the east. Only the *Santa Maria* and the *Nina* were left together. Columbus continued to explore Cuba before heading east and

Pineapples (far left), tobacco plants (left) and parrots (below) were some of the wonders brought back to Spain by Columbus.

arriving at Hispaniola, which means the Spanish Island. Here Columbus made friends with a local chief named Guacanagari.

In the early hours of Christmas Day, the *Santa Maria* ran onto a reef. Although she did not sink, the ship was so badly damaged it was clear that she could not make the voyage back to Spain. With the help of Guacanagari and his men, Columbus transferred the stores and equipment of the *Santa Maria* to shore. The tiny *Nina* could not carry both crews back to Spain, so Columbus decided to build a fort and leave some of his men there. Guacanagari and the local people were friendly and crops grew freely. It seemed that they would find it easy to survive there.

Timbers from the *Santa Maria* were used to build the fort, which was named La Navidad. Weapons from the ship were brought ashore, in case trouble did occur. Columbus demonstrated the power of the cannon by demolishing a distant tree with a single shot. While work on the fort continued, many local people came to trade with the Spaniards. They brought gold jewelery to swap for cheap bells, clothes and ribbons. Columbus was delighted. He had heard tales of rich gold mines some distance away and he decided that China could not be far away. But he realized that his most important task was to return home. The *Pinta* had disappeared and the *Santa Maria* was wrecked. Unless Columbus reached Spain safely, his great discoveries would be useless. All that would be known would be that the ships had vanished into the western ocean. Columbus sadly turned his back on the men at La Navidad and the possibility of reaching China.

The Voyage Home

On January 4, having provided La Navidad with as many provisions and guns as he could, Columbus set sail for home. He decided to follow the coast of Hispaniola eastward as far as possible. On the third day of sailing, the lookout spotted a European ship on the horizon to the northwest. It was the *Pinta*.

The *Pinta* sailed quickly to meet the *Nina*. As soon as the ships were close enough, Martin Pinzon rowed a small boat across to speak to Columbus. He apologized for leaving the *Santa Maria*, but said that the *Pinta* had been caught in a fast tidal stream, which he was not able to sail against. Columbus, however, did not believe Pinzon. Some of the sailors on the *Pinta* said that Pinzon had heard about a gold mine. Columbus thought Pinzon had deliberately sailed away to raid this gold mine. However, he pretended to trust Pinzon as he could not afford any trouble to occur during the voyage home.

The two ships continued to sail along the coast of Hispaniola. Before finally setting out for home, they took on fresh water, lumber and fruit. One day, the sailors came across large numbers of turtles and sea cows, or manatees, which they decided were mermaids. With these wonders noted in his log, Columbus

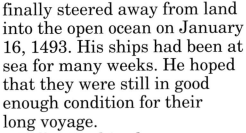

Left Columbus found large numbers of turtles on the islands he visited.

Below On the voyage home, the Pinta *and* Nina *were struck by a terrible storm and became separated. Each crew thought that the other ship had been sunk.*

finally steered away from land into the open ocean on January 16, 1493. His ships had been at sea for many weeks. He hoped that they were still in good enough condition for their long voyage.

Following his plan, Columbus steered northeast to catch the easterly winds. For nearly a month the voyage went well. But on February 12, a strong southerly wind blew up. By nightfall the weather had changed for the worse. A terrific storm raged and mountainous waves crashed over the decks of the ships. The wind was so fierce that all the sails had to be taken down so that the masts would not blow away. During the night, both ships lit large lanterns so that they could stay together. But in the early hours of the morning, the lights of the *Pinta* vanished. Columbus and the *Nina* were left alone.

Columbus decided that only God could help. The entire crew prayed, promising that if they survived to reach land they would walk barefoot to the nearest church and offer thanks to God. Columbus promised to visit the shrine of Santa Maria de Guadelupe.

The storm did not die down, so Columbus wrote down a brief account of his voyage, sealed it in a barrel and threw it overboard. He hoped that if the ship sank, somebody would find the barrel and read about the voyage. Eventually, after two days, the storm died down.

On February 15, 1493, Columbus sighted the Azores. These islands were owned by Portugal, and Columbus would have preferred to avoid them. But the *Nina* was so badly damaged that Columbus was forced to stop at St. Mary's harbor for repairs. Columbus and his men set out barefoot to keep their promise to God. The first group of sailors had just reached the church when they were arrested. Columbus was furious. Only after much talking and threats did he persuade the local governor to free his men. Putting to sea again, the *Nina* was caught in a second storm.

A Wonderful Welcome

At dawn on March 4, the second storm died down and Columbus found himself off the Portuguese coast. After his experiences in the Azores, Columbus did not want to land. But nearly all his sails had been ripped by the wind, and the *Nina* was in a terrible condition. Columbus sailed into the Tagus River and asked for workmen to repair his ship.

Columbus need not have worried. King John of Portugal sent orders that the *Nina* was to be repaired and stores provided free of charge. He also asked Columbus to visit the court and tell everybody about his voyage. Still fearing a trap, Columbus traveled to Lisbon. Here he found himself in great demand. He was invited to parties and banquets

Below Columbus and his men walked in procession to display the treasures they had brought back from their voyage.

where everybody wanted to hear about his voyage. King John wanted to make sure that Columbus had not been secretly exploring Africa. On March 13, Columbus left Portugal and two days later he sailed into Palos, in Spain.

When he arrived, the town celebrated wildly. All the stores and businesses were shut as the people crowded down to the docks. A fiesta was declared and the whole city joined in a party. The celebrations lasted until dawn. Columbus sent a long letter to King Ferdinand and Queen Isabella. Their reply commanded him to go to their court at Barcelona. The royal letter addressed Columbus as Viceroy, Admiral and Governor. Columbus was receiving his rewards.

Soon after Columbus' return to Palos, the *Pinta* also sailed into port. Captain Pinzon and his crew had been swept far to the north during a storm and had reached France at about the same time that Columbus had sailed into the Tagus River. Pinzon was not to enjoy any reward for his successful return. He was extremely ill and died a few days after returning to Spain.

Columbus, meanwhile, had traveled to Barcelona. He entered the city with a great procession. Sailors carried treasures through the streets from the lands they had visited. These included gold and jewels, caged parrots, stuffed animals, pineapples, strange plants and six of the men Columbus had called Indians. The streets were crowded with people and even the rooftops were covered with spectators. Ferdinand and Isabella met Columbus in the palace. They listened as Columbus showed them his finds and described the voyage.

Columbus was given many honors and rewards. He was immediately awarded a huge sum of money to make a second voyage. First, however, Spain and Portugal needed to reach an agreement as to which nation owned these new territories. Columbus' discoveries would be ruled by Spain, while Africa would be ruled by Portugal. In the Treaty of Tordesillas, signed by Spanish and Portuguese ambassadors in 1494, a dividing line running from north to south about 1,700 km (1,056 mi) west of Cape Verde was agreed upon. Any new countries discovered west of the line were to be Spanish, and those to the east were to belong to Portugal. Other seagoing countries, such as England and France, were left out of this agreement; they refused to accept it as a legal document and this was to lead to much trouble in the future.

The Second Voyage

On May 24, 1493, Columbus was given instructions from the monarchs about his coming voyage. The main purpose of the expedition was to set up a trading colony at the site of his earlier fort, La Navidad. This settlement was to trade with the local people for gold, cotton, spices and other goods. Only when this had been achieved would Columbus continue his search for China and Japan.

Within a few weeks, Columbus had collected together a fleet of 17 ships and 1,500 men. Many of the men had been persuaded to sign on by stories of gold and spices. Their greed was to cause trouble later. Columbus' fleet sailed from Cadiz in Spain on September 25, 1493. After a short stop at the Canaries, the ships made a fast and trouble-free voyage across the ocean.

On November 3, Columbus sighted the island of Dominica. This is part of a group in the West Indies, now known as the Windward Islands. Columbus landed several times on the islands in this group and was horrified at what he found. In several villages he saw human flesh cooking on fires. The local people were cannibals. Columbus' crew managed to rescue several prisoners, from whom they learned that these cannibals were called Caribs. From this term comes the name of the Caribbean Sea and that of its islands.

After sailing through these islands for several days, Columbus reached Hispaniola and coasted on to La Navidad. Disaster awaited him. While he had been away, a fierce tribal war had broken out. The Spanish crew members Columbus had left there had become involved. They had been massacred and only the empty walls of La Navidad remained. Columbus founded a second settlement nearby and named it Isabella. The local people led by Guacanagari remained loyal, but other groups attacked the Spaniards. The Spaniards defeated them but also suffered many casualties of their own in the fighting.

Below *The rugged coast of Hispaniola, where Columbus established his first colony in the New World.*

When the war died down, Columbus set out to sail westward and look for China. He left Pedro Margarit in command at Isabella. For several weeks, in April 1494, Columbus sailed along the coast of Cuba. After covering 1,200 km (746 mi), Columbus turned back. He then forced his entire crew to swear that they had found Asia and that China had been only a short distance farther on. It was becoming clear, even to Columbus who did not want to admit he was wrong, that they had not reached China.

On his return to the settlement of Isabella, Columbus found more trouble. Disease had broken out, the colony was at war with the local people, and many of the colonists were discontented with Columbus' rules and laws. Bartolomeo Columbus arrived from Spain and helped him to bring order to Isabella. However, several colonists had sailed for Spain, carrying reports of corruption and mismanagement. In the spring of 1496, Columbus decided to sail for Spain to defend himself against these charges.

Above *The early Spanish settlers became involved in fierce wars between the local people and suffered heavy casualties.*

Later Journeys

When he arrived back in Spain, Columbus was able to explain the difficulties at Isabella. His critics were defeated, but they had gained powerful friends. Many people in Spain were jealous of Columbus. He had arrived as a penniless foreigner and had now become rich and famous and friendly with the king and queen. His enemies began to plot against him.

In 1498 Columbus set sail for Isabella. He was to be governor again. This time he was ordered by Ferdinand and Isabella to try to convert the local people to Christianity and employ them as workers on farms run by Spaniards. The farms were to grow sugar, cotton and other valuable crops. However, many Spaniards were not interested in farming. They wanted to steal gold and valuables, make a quick profit and return to Spain. Columbus did his best to deal with the problems. After more than a year, he had the situation under control. He sent a message to Spain asking for administrators to help him run the colony.

The man appointed to help him was Francisco de Bobadilla, a nobleman who was a government officer. Bobadilla disliked foreigners and wealthy commoners, and both these groups included

Above As Governor of Isabella, Columbus became an enemy of an important official named Francisco de Bobadilla, who sent him back to Spain in chains. Columbus was later released and made another voyage to the New World.

Columbus. Bobadilla had been given powers to arrest corrupt officials and send them back to Spain. The monarchs had intended this power to be used to suppress rebellion, but Bobadilla turned against Columbus. He imprisoned Columbus in iron manacles and put him on a ship sailing for Spain.

When he arrived at the Spanish court, Columbus persuaded the monarchs to free him. However, they refused to send him back to Isabella as governor. Though denied power, Columbus was still receiving plenty of money. He was given one tenth of government profits and was allowed to partly finance trading expeditions.

In 1502, Columbus made a fourth voyage across the Atlantic. On this journey he discovered and mapped large sections of the coast of Central America. Though he still thought that he had reached Asia, Columbus was forced to admit he had not discovered a route to China or Japan. Columbus returned to Spain a disappointed man. Queen Isabella had died and the new King Philip, who had never met Columbus, mistrusted him. He preferred to believe his government ministers, who jealously accused Columbus of mismanagement. Columbus died on May 20, 1506. For some years his children tried to regain the honors they felt were owed to him by the government. Eventually, the Columbus family was rewarded.

Below *A map showing the routes of Columbus' four voyages to the New World.*

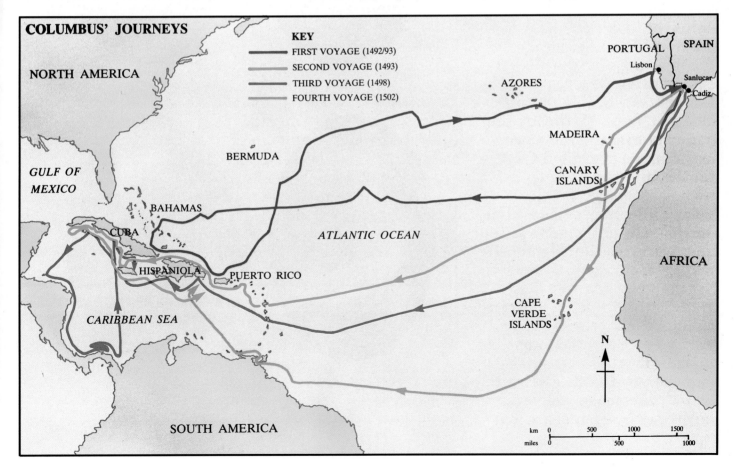

The New World

When Christopher Columbus died in 1506 he believed that he had found a westward route to Asia. Many other people in Europe shared this belief, but others disagreed. As more and more lands were discovered and explored, the vast size of the islands and coasts became clear. China and Japan could not, however, be found. It was becoming clear that Columbus had reached a new continent.

At one point Columbus had thought that this might be the case. On his third voyage he found the Orinoco River, which was so large it could only have come from a large continent. Columbus wrote that he felt this continent could not be China, but later he changed his mind. The first man to publicize the idea that Columbus had not reached Asia was the Italian mariner Amerigo Vespucci. During the sixteenth century, the new continent he identified was named Amerigo, or America, in his honor.

The difficulties of governing the Spanish settlements in the New World continued after the death of Columbus. Colonists and merchants traveled across the Atlantic for many different reasons. Some journeyed to start a new life, others to make quick profits. A large number were sent by the government to run the colonies and bring wealth to Spain. Disease and slavery reduced the numbers of local people on the Caribbean islands, but sickness also killed many Spaniards. Though profitable, the colonies in the Caribbean remained relatively unimportant to Spain for many years.

Later explorers who visited the New World were more interested in money than exploration.
1. Hernando Cortés;
2. Francisco Pizarro;
3. Sir John Hawkins;
4. Sir Francis Drake.

1.

2.

3.

4.

Then, in 1519, Hernando Cortés discovered and conquered the fabulously wealthy Aztec Empire, in what is now Mexico. Thousands of settlers and government officials sailed to Mexico and the Caribbean. In 1532, Francisco Pizarro claimed the Inca Empire in South America for Spain, and its gold and silver mines produced many treasures. Trading with the Spanish settlements became increasingly profitable. The government in Madrid imposed heavy taxes on this trade in order to gain huge profits.

Soon other nations began to be interested in America. The Treaty of Tordesillas had not been signed by nations other than Spain and Portugal. To the north of the Spanish colonies, other settlements began to appear. British travelers settled along the coast of North America, beside Dutch and French colonies.

Ships from England, France and Germany began to trade with the Spanish colonies. These merchants paid no taxes to Madrid, so the Spanish navy was ordered to sink any non-Spanish ships on sight if they dared to cross the boundary decided upon in the Treaty of Tordesillas. Any unauthorized persons who were caught were thrown into prison or tortured. This began a long-running series of raids on Spanish colonies in which Englishmen such as Sir Francis Drake and Sir John Hawkins became rich and famous.

As the years passed, the true importance of Columbus' voyages emerged. He had reached a previously unknown continent that was rich in both treasures and fertile land. Today millions of people who are descended from European settlers live in both North and South America. The United States has become one of the richest and most powerful nations in the world.

Above This painting shows Hernando Cortés and his men fighting the Aztecs.

Below A map produced in 1500, which shows the lands that had been visited by Spanish explorers up to that date. The two large islands in the center are Cuba and Hispaniola.

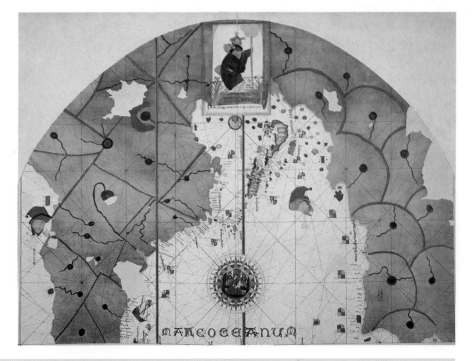

Glossary

Admiral A senior naval officer who commands a fleet of ships or a navy.

Atlantis A continent believed, in ancient legend, to have sunk beneath the Atlantic Ocean.

Bow The front of a ship.

Caravel A type of sailing ship commonly used by merchants in the fifteenth century.

Circumference The distance around the outside of a circle or sphere.

Corruption Dishonest action in which an official is paid money, or bribed, to make a particular decision.

Decree An official order or command.

Fiesta A traditional Spanish party. Every person in a town or village attends and many bring along something to eat or drink.

Geographer Someone who studies the natural features of the Earth's surface.

Log The daily record of a voyage or flight kept by the captain of a ship or plane.

Manacles Chains used to tie prisoners' hands or feet together to keep them from escaping.

Moor A member of a Muslim people of North Africa, who ruled large areas of Spain during the Middle Ages.

Pilgrimage A journey made to visit a shrine or a sacred place.

Rudder cable A length of thick rope that controlled the rudder, and therefore the steering, of caravels and other sailing ships.

Sphere A round, three-dimensional shape.

Stern The back part of a ship.

Theory An idea not necessarily based on fact, that is put forward to explain a certain problem or situation.

Trinket An inexpensive, brightly colored object such as a bracelet or ring.

Viceroy Someone who is appointed by a monarch to rule an area of land. A viceroy has all the powers of the monarch.

Picture Acknowledgments

The publishers would like to thank the following for their illustrations:

Aldus Archive 5, 6 (top), 20 (top left); Ancient Art & Architecture Collection 7 (top and bottom), 17; Bridgeman Art Library 8, 28 (bottom left and right; by courtesy of the Crown Estate with the cooperation of the Institute of Directors); Chapel Studios *frontispiece*; Bruce Coleman 19 (top right), 24; E.T. Archive 19 (top left), 29 (top and bottom); Mary Evans 4, 6, 9 (top), 11, 28 (top right); Michael Holford 4, 9 (bottom), 19 (bottom); Tony Stone Picture Library 12 (top), 18 (top); Topham 20 (top). All maps by Peter Bull.

Finding out More

You may find it interesting to try to find out more about how European settlements developed and what happened to the original people in the locality. Subjects to look for in your local library include Colonial America, the Aztecs, the Incas, the Spanish Empire and the Caribbean Islands.

There are no surviving ships from the time of Columbus, but many museums contain models of the type of ship he used and the equipment and weapons used by sailors at that time.

Books to Read

Your local library should be able to help you to find some of these books.

Penny Bateman, *Aztecs and Incas*. Franklin Watts, 1988
Barbara Beck, *The Aztecs*. Franklin Watts, 1983
Allan Blackwood, *Ferdinand Magellan*. Bookwright, 1986
Nathaniel Harris, *Montezuma and the Aztecs*. Bookwright, 1986

Jill Hughes, *Aztecs*. Gloucester, 1986
Richard Humble, *The Voyage of Magellan*. Franklin Watts, 1989
Anne Millard, *The Incas*. Warwick, 1980
Marion Morrison, *Atahuallpa and the Incas*. Bookwright, 1986
Gardner Soule, *Christopher Columbus on the Green Sea of Darkness*. Franklin Watts, 1988
Cass Sandak, *Explorers and Discovery*. Franklin Watts, 1983

Index